UNDERGROUND CITY SYSTEMS

Ellen Rodger

CRABTREE
PUBLISHING COMPANY
WWW.CRABTREEBOOKS.COM

CRABTREE
PUBLISHING COMPANY
WWW.CRABTREEBOOKS.COM

Author: Ellen Rodger

Editorial Director: Kathy Middleton

Editors: Petrice Custance, Sonya Newland

Proofreaders: Lorna Notsch, Ellen Rodger

Designer: Steve Mead

Cover design: Tammy McGarr

**Production coordinator and
    Prepress technician:** Tammy McGarr

Print coordinator: Katherine Berti

Produced for Crabtree Publishing Company
by White-Thomson Publishing Ltd

Photographs

Cover: Alamy: Joern Sackermann (left); All other images from
Shutterstock

Interior: Alamy: 4 (Thomas Henrikson), 5 (MS Bretherton), 8–9 (Bill
Brooks), 16–17 (Joern Sackerman), 17 (volkerpreusser), 18 (Granger
Historical Picture Archive), 19 (Richard Levine), 23 (Niday Picture
Library); Julian Baker: 7, 22, 24, 26–27; Getty Images: 10–11 (Corbis
Historical), 14 (Heritage Images), 15 (Adrian Dennis), 20–21 (Ronaldo
Scheimidt), 25 (Dick Loek), 28 (Daniel Leal-Olivas); Shutterstock: 6
(josefkubes), 8 (Alan Linn), 11 (FCG), 12 (Morphart Creation), 13 (Styve
Reineck), 20 (kai hecker), 27 (Erin Cadigan), 29 (Aisyaqilumaranas).

Library and Archives Canada Cataloguing in Publication

Rodger, Ellen, author
        Underground city systems / Ellen Rodger.

(Underground worlds)
Includes index.
Issued in print and electronic formats.
ISBN 978-0-7787-6081-8 (hardcover).--
ISBN 978-0-7787-6163-1 (softcover).--
ISBN 978-1-4271-2250-6 (HTML)

        1. Underground utility lines--Juvenile literature. 2. Sewerage--
Juvenile literature. I. Title.

TD168.R63 2018   j628   C2018-905528-6
                                              C2018-905529-4

Library of Congress Cataloging-in-Publication Data

Names: Rodger, Ellen, author.
Title: Underground city systems / Ellen Rodger.
Description: New York, New York : Crabtree Publishing, 2019. |
    Series: Underground worlds | Includes index.
Identifiers: LCCN 2018043798 (print) | LCCN 2018045427 (ebook) |
    ISBN 9781427122506 (Electronic) |
    ISBN 9780778760818 (hardcover) |
    ISBN 9780778761631 (pbk.)
Subjects: LCSH: Underground utility lines--Juvenile literature.
Classification: LCC TD168 (ebook) | LCC TD168 .R63 2019 (print) |
    DDC 628--dc23
LC record available at https://lccn.loc.gov/2018043798

Crabtree Publishing Company

www.crabtreebooks.com   1-800-387-7650

Printed in the U.S.A./122018/CG20181005

Published in Canada
Crabtree Publishing
616 Welland Ave.
St. Catharines, Ontario
L2M 5V6

Published in the United States
Crabtree Publishing
PMB 59051
350 Fifth Avenue, 59th Floor
New York, New York 10118

Published in the United Kingdom
Crabtree Publishing
Maritime House
Basin Road North, Hove
BN41 1WR

Published in Australia
Crabtree Publishing
3 Charles Street
Coburg North
VIC, 3058

CONTENTS

WHAT LIES BENEATH?

When you stroll along the sidewalks of your city or town, do you ever think of what lies beneath your feet? Is there a 60-mile (97-km) long water tunnel, such as the one in New York City? What about a big blob of fat and sewage waste, such as the fatberg in London, England?

Sewers and Pipes

Almost all modern cities and towns have underground tunnels, pipes, water, and **sewage systems**. The water that comes out of our faucets flows through these underground systems. They also allow us to flush our toilets and use electricity every day without much of a thought.

▽ Some underground sewage tunnels are large enough to paddle through in a canoe.

DID YOU KNOW?

Before underground sewers, people in **medieval** Europe dumped their **chamber pots** out their windows and into the street!

Ancient Underground Systems

The complex underground city systems that exist today are the result of thousands of years of experiments. The earliest drainage systems were built in 6000 B.C.E. in the ancient cities of the Indus River Valley, in what is now Pakistan. They were designed to flush household water into chutes that led to street drains. Unlike sewers today, these were aboveground. They were basically covered drains for wastewater, or water that has been used for washing or sewage.

By the 1800s, indoor plumbing had been developed, and cities built their sewers underground, where they wouldn't be seen. Eventually, other city systems joined the sewers underground. Today, there are power cables and gas lines beneath our feet wherever we go in a built-up area. In some cities, farms even grow food underground!

△ Construction on the Crossness **Pumping Station** in London was completed in 1865. It was known for its beautiful decorative ironwork. Today, it is a museum.

5

TAP TO TREATMENT PLANT

When you turn on your bathroom or kitchen taps, clean water flows out. And when you flush your toilet, dirty water disappears. But where does that water come from, and where does it go?

Tap Water

The tap water we drink and use to wash ourselves, or do the dishes and laundry, comes from nearby lakes or rivers. Some cities get water from underground pockets called **aquifers**. The water from these sources is cleaned, or "treated." Treating water removes harmful **bacteria** that could make people sick. The water is then pumped through a main line and miles of smaller underground pipes to your home.

▽ At a water treatment plant, the water is kept in huge storage tanks.

Wastewater

So where does your waste go when you flush your toilet, or your washing machine drains? If your home is connected to the city sewer system, it gets pushed through pipes that lead to the water treatment plant. At the plant, the waste is filtered and solids are removed. The wastewater is then treated with **chemicals** to clean it. The cleaned water is stored in a **reservoir** or put back into rivers and lakes.

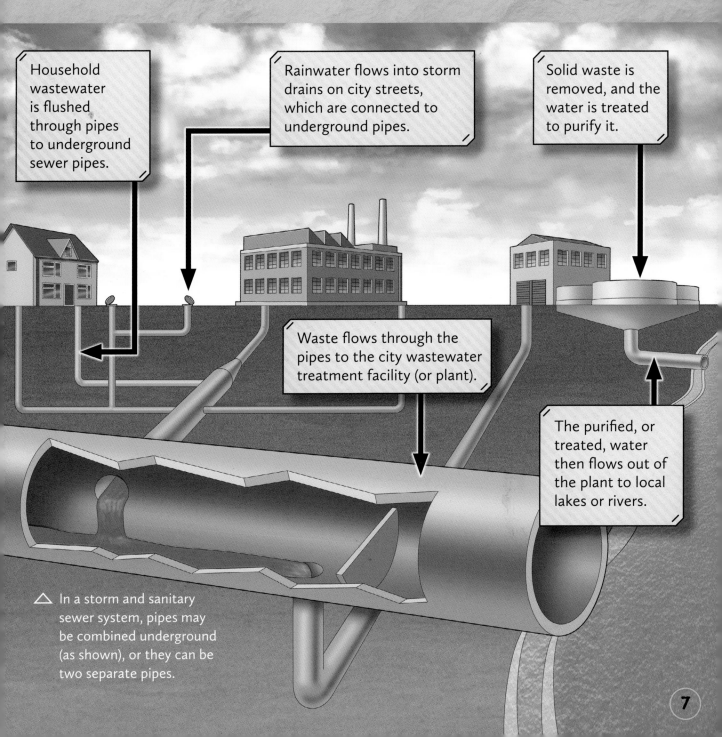

Household wastewater is flushed through pipes to underground sewer pipes.

Rainwater flows into storm drains on city streets, which are connected to underground pipes.

Solid waste is removed, and the water is treated to purify it.

Waste flows through the pipes to the city wastewater treatment facility (or plant).

The purified, or treated, water then flows out of the plant to local lakes or rivers.

△ In a storm and sanitary sewer system, pipes may be combined underground (as shown), or they can be two separate pipes.

Storm Drains

Most city streets and sidewalks are paved over with concrete or asphalt cement. They do not allow rainwater to seep into the ground the way soil does. This is why we have storm drains.

When it rains, water runs down the pavement into the storm drain. The water collects and flows through pipes to the nearest water body, such as a local stream, river, or lake.

◁ That storm drain on the street near your home helps to prevent flooding in your city.

Overflow

Combined sewers are city sewer systems combined with storm drains. These sometimes overflow. This happens when heavy rainfall or snowmelt sends too much water into the sewage system. These sewage overflows send stormwater and untreated waste into nearby waterways. An estimated 23,000 to 75,000 overflows happen in the U.S. each year. Stormwater can carry all sorts of pollution, such as cigarette butts, pet waste, and household cleaners.

▽ In Flin Flon, water and sewage pipes are concealed in boxes on the surface.

DID YOU KNOW?

Flin Flon in Manitoba, Canada, may be one of the only cities in the world with aboveground water and sewage lines. The mining city is built on **bedrock** that made it impossible to bury the lines. Heated water circulates in the lines to prevent freezing in winter.

SEWERS OF PARIS

The sewers in Paris, France, have a long and colorful history. Parts of the network date back to 1370, but real underground work began in 1800, when the French leader Napoleon Bonaparte made building more sewer tunnels a part of his plan to modernize the city.

Disappearing Underground

Napoleon sent an explorer to map the old tunnels, and he reportedly found lost jewels and the skeleton of an orangutan that had escaped from a zoo! The sewers were properly expanded in 1850, after diseases caused by polluted water killed thousands of people in Paris. Engineer Eugene Belgrand designed large tunnels, big enough to stand up in. They were even named like city streets. The new system supplied water and removed waste. By 1878, there were 373 miles (600 km) of sewer lines underneath Paris. For the first time, houses had direct sewer hookups.

This illustration shows a part of the Paris sewer being built. Originally just 3 miles (5 km) long, it was designed to carry waste to the Seine River.

Here Come the Sewermen

The new sewers brought a new type of job: sewer cleaners. These cleaners, or "sewermen," worked underground in the sewer tunnels. They used **sluice gates,** carts, and boats to help the sewage flow along. Sewermen also raked the muck and used enormous wooden or metal balls to flatten blockages.

△ The Paris sewers still operate today. Machinery is used to clear debris from the tunnels so they don't get clogged.

DID YOU KNOW?

The Paris sewers are mentioned in books, including *Les Misérables* and *The Phantom of the Opera*. In these books, the sewers provide a place to hide from danger.

Take a Tour!

Tourists have been taking tours through Paris's sewers since 1867. Early on, people rode through the sewers in a wagon. From 1920 until 1975, tourists could float through on boats. Visitors reported that the sewer tunnels were quite clean, with only a whiff of the usual sewer odor. Today, there are still walking tours of sewers during which people can learn how solid waste is **dredged** out.

▽ This illustration shows sewermen pulling tourists through the underground mazes of Paris's sewers.

Visit a Museum!

Since sewers are an important city service, some cities also have sewer museums. At the Paris Sewer Museum, visitors can learn about the things sewer workers find in the sewers, such as keys and jewelry. They keep these finds, unless someone has reported them missing. There are also sewer museums in Brussels, Belgium, and Tokyo, Japan.

The Paris Catacombs

Paris's sewers are not the city's only underground fascination. People like to visit the catacombs, too. These burial grounds are packed with the remains of six million people. They were created in the 1770s, when the city's cemeteries became too full.

OSSEMENTS DE L'ANCIEN CIMETIÈRE DE LA MAGDELEINE (RUE DE LA VILLE LÉVÈQUE Nos 1 et 2) DÉPOSÉS EN 1844 DANS L'OSSUAIRE DE L'OUEST ET TRANSFÉRÉS DANS LES CATACOMBES EN SEPTEMBRE 1859.

△ The tunnel walls in the catacombs are made of bones.

DID YOU KNOW?

In 1904, a photographer and a journalist began exploring the sewers of Vienna, Austria. They published a book on the homeless men who lived in the sewer's tunnels, who they called "molemen."

LONDON'S SEWERS

In London, the summer of 1858 was boiling hot. Raw sewage and **slaughterhouse** waste steamed and crusted on the banks of the Thames River. The smell was so bad that it became known as the "Great Stink." The polluted water was also causing killer diseases such as **cholera**.

Dangerous Water

To solve the problem, engineer Sir Joseph Bazalgette was asked to build a sewer system. The system used four pumping stations and two treatment plants. Completed in 1870, Bazalgette's underground system was an amazing feat of engineering. There were also three **embankments** to help prevent backups when heavy rains flooded the sewers. The new sewers saved lives by separating drinking water from sewage water. This prevented major outbreaks of disease.

◁ Workers dug out 82 miles (132 km) of main sewer lines and 1,100 miles (1,770 km) of street sewers.

Miles of Pipe

The old sewers are still in use, but today they make up only one percent of London's sewage network. Today, a huge super-sewer system is being built to carry waste and water throughout the city. The Thames Tideway Tunnel will run 16 miles (25 km) under the River Thames.

Great Ball of Guck

There are still problems, though. In 2017, a huge blockage was removed from a London sewer by workers using shovels and hoses. Nicknamed "fatberg," it was made up of 143 tons (130 metric tons) of dumped diapers, cooking grease, and other garbage. The fatberg was placed on display at the London Museum. This fatberg isn't the only one. Sewage systems all over the world get plugged with debris people flush down the toilet.

◁ Fatbergs are as solid as concrete. They smell really bad.

COLOGNE, GERMANY

Imagine hanging a chandelier in a sewer! There is an underground sewer hall in Cologne, Germany, that includes a setting fit for royalty.

The plaque reads:

AUSGEFÜHRT
UNTER DEM OBERBÜRGERMEISTER
W. BECKER
UND DEM STADTBAURAT
J. STÜBBEN
DURCH DEN STADTBAUINSPECTOR
C. STEUERNAGEL
IM JAHRE 1890
BAULEITUNG INGENIEUR
H. BERGER

BAUUNTERNEHMER:
E.A. MENZEL

Foul Air

In the early 1800s, Cologne was described as having "two and seventy stenches, all well defined, and several stinks!" In that respect, it wasn't much different from other big cities with no sewers. The city's smelly waste **festered** in open ditches.

Preparing for the Emperor

Finally, in 1890, an underground sewage system was built. Everyone thought that the emperor, Wilhelm II, would attend the opening ceremony. So, to make the sewer special, workers installed a 12-armed candle chandelier in one of the tunnel chambers. The emperor didn't show up, but the chandelier stayed. It was eventually replaced with an electric chandelier.

△ The old Roman sewers beneath the streets of Cologne.

▽ The chamber containing the chandelier is sometimes used for small classical music concerts. Sewage no longer flows into this section of the tunnel.

Roman Wonder

Cologne is home to another sewage system—one that was built nearly 2,000 years ago by the Romans. The tunnels were forgotten for centuries until a German **architect** rediscovered them in 1830. For years after, they were used to store beer. During **World War II**, people used them as shelters during **air raids**. Today, **archaeologists** are still finding new tunnels that are part of this ancient system.

DID YOU KNOW?

Cologne now has more than 1,250 miles (2,000 km) of sewer tunnels running under the city. Five treatment plants clean the water before dumping it into the Rhine River.

SEWERS OF
NEW YORK CITY

With a population of 8.5 million, New York is the biggest city in the United States. It also has an extensive system of underground sewer and water lines with 6,000 miles (9,656 km) of pipes.

Creepy Underbelly

Sewer dwellers, monsters, and muck—NYC's sewers are the stuff of legend. One of the most popular legends is that homeless people live in them. They don't, as the sewers are much too wet and dangerous. There are also no monsters, or alligators, and the rats do not outnumber the people. NYC's rat population is about two million. The most dangerous thing about the system is sewer gas, which is a mix of gases produced when waste matter **decomposes**. It contains carbon monoxide, which can kill at high doses.

DID YOU KNOW?

If you flush it, sewer workers might find it! In NYC, workers at treatment plants have found all sorts of things, including Christmas trees, stuffed animals, and real animals (sometimes still alive).

▽ This carving in a sewage disposal plant in New York commemorates the men who built the sewage system in the 1850s.

A Watery World

Much of New York City is located on land that used to be forest.
Many streams and springs ran through the area. These ancient
waterways are still there, although they are now covered with
buildings and sidewalks. Because the springs still drip through
underground tunnels, the brickwork of these tunnels has to be
constantly monitored and repaired.

Modern Systems

New York has had an underground sewer system since the 1850s.
It originally carried untreated waste out to the East River. Today,
the city's treatment plants manage 1.3 billion gallons (4.9 billion
liters) of wastewater a day. Raw sewage is still sometimes dumped
into the river when there is a bad storm or a power outage.

WORKING IN SEWERS

Imagine the grossest job anyone could possibly have. Does sewer worker come to mind? What about upping the gross level with sewer diving? Most people don't even know what sewer workers do, or that sewer divers exist.

Soaking It In

The entrances into sewers are sealed by heavy manhole covers. They are there to keep street garbage—and people—out of the sewers. Sewer workers hook and heave up the covers, then climb down into the tunnels to inspect pipes and make sure things are running smoothly. They wear rubber boots and long waterproof trousers called hip waders to protect them in the filthy water.

DID YOU KNOW?

Sewer divers have air tanks, so they don't smell the sewage or get hit with sewer gas. They also get so used to the smell at sewer sites, that they don't notice it anymore.

◁ Manhole covers typically weigh between 100 and 200 pounds (45 to 91 kg).

Diving through What?

Sewer divers are a special kind of sewer worker. It's their job to clear debris from clogged tunnels or pumps. Deep in the sewer water, it is too dark for them to see, so they have to feel their way around. They dress head-to-toe in diving gear, equipped with oxygen. Their protective helmets have microphones so they can communicate with other workers. Members of a team are linked by a cord so they don't get lost in the mucky, watery goo. Sometimes, the divers use **suction** equipment to break down blockages. Other times, they pull out garbage, dead animals, tires, or car parts with their hands.

▽ Mexico City has two sewer divers, who dive about four days per month.

USEFUL UTILIDORS

Do you know what's going on under your street right now? There may be cables buried under your garden, passing information faster than the blink of an eye. Or what about a tunnel for electrical and other services beneath your apartment building?

Other Underground Services

The word "utilidor" is a combination of "**utility**" and "corridor." It is the name given to an underground passageway or tunnel that serves a useful purpose. Usually, many different utility lines, such as telephone and cable lines, run through utilidors. In some cities, electrical cables may have protective coverings or pipes, but elsewhere they may be buried under the ground without them. Utilities are buried for many reasons, such as to protect them from storms that down trees and lines, or because too many utility poles are considered unattractive.

▽ Underground home utilities

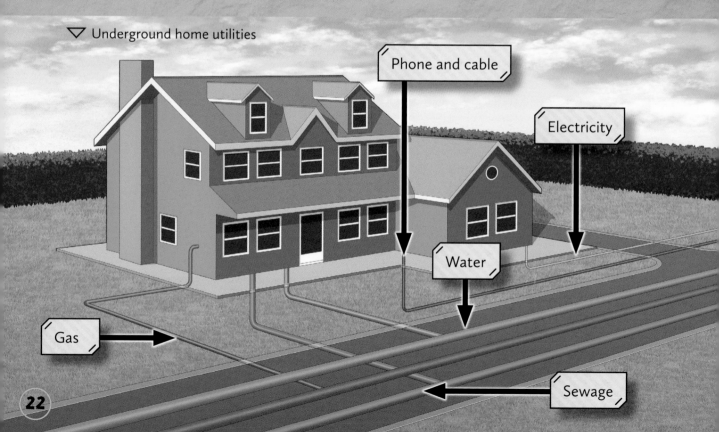

Phone and cable

Electricity

Water

Gas

Sewage

△ After the Illinois Telegraph and Telephone Company closed down, the Chicago Tunnel Company began using the underground network for moving goods beneath the city.

Chicago's Underground

A century ago, a system of delivery tunnels operated deep beneath Chicago's downtown. They were built to deliver goods and coal. The goods were sold in stores or used in offices. The coal was used to heat the buildings. Originally, the tunnels were supposed to be just for telephones and telegraph lines. But the company that built them made them larger—enough for small trains to fit through. The tunnels were in operation until 1959.

DID YOU KNOW?

Disney theme parks are like cities in their own right. They have their own underground systems and services. Utilidors under the parks hide the water and electricity services.

UNDERWATER COOLING

Summers in Toronto, Canada, can be hot and steamy. It takes a lot of energy to air-condition the big buildings in the city's downtown. Since the early 2000s, an underground system of piped cold water from nearby Lake Ontario has been used to keep many buildings cool.

Deep-Water Cooling

Toronto lies on the north shore of Lake Ontario. The water here is 279 feet (85 m) deep less than 3.1 miles (5 km) from shore. The deep-water cooling project uses water from deep in the lake, where the temperature is 39.2° F (4° C) year-round. The system works by using a **heat exchanger** at a city water pumping station. The cold water's energy replaces air-conditioning created through electricity or **fossil fuels**.

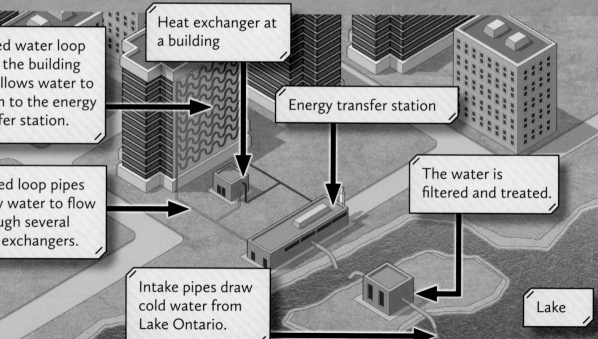

Chilled water loop cools the building and allows water to return to the energy transfer station.

Heat exchanger at a building

Energy transfer station

The water is filtered and treated.

Closed loop pipes allow water to flow through several heat exchangers.

Intake pipes draw cold water from Lake Ontario.

Lake

▽ Cooling pipes about to be sunk below the surface of Lake Ontario

DID YOU KNOW?

The deep-water cooling system uses three 3-mile (5-km) pipes to collect water. The water used to cool buildings is the same source water used for Toronto's drinking supply.

Toronto Is Chill

Several major Toronto buildings are cooled by water pumped from the depths of the lake. They include City Hall, Mount Sinai Hospital, and a brewery. Scotiabank Arena, home to the Toronto Raptors basketball team and the Toronto Maple Leafs hockey team, is also cooled this way.

PNEUMATIC NEW YORK

Underground tubes that vacuum garbage out of buildings in one place and deposit it in another sound like something out of a science-fiction movie. But the system exists in real life—and it could be the model for the future of city garbage removal.

Island of Sucked Garbage

Roosevelt Island is a narrow strip of land on the East River in Manhattan, New York. The 2-mile (3.2-km) long island is home to about 14,000 people. Everyone lives in apartments. The residents put their garbage in chutes located on their floors inside the building. The trash is then sucked down tubes to a giant container, instead of being collected on the curb and hauled away by trucks.

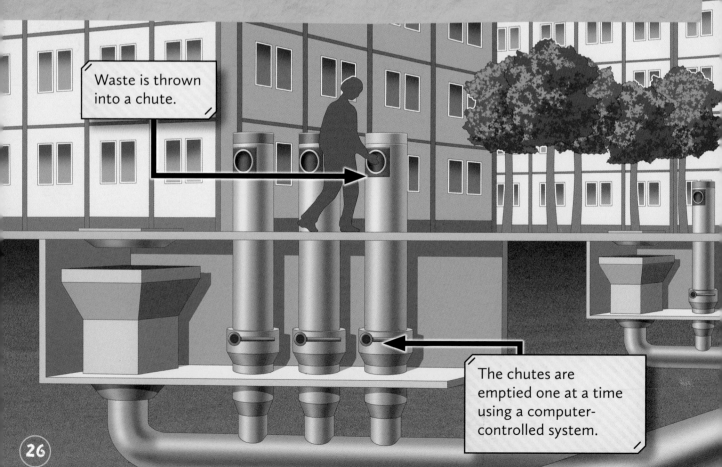

Waste is thrown into a chute.

The chutes are emptied one at a time using a computer-controlled system.

In other parts of New York, trash is collected and transported by barge to disposal venues.

Underground Trash

The tubes, called **pneumatic** tubes, use air pressure to move the garbage at 65 miles an hour (105 kph). Each day, 6 tons (5.4 metric tons) of trash are moved to huge containers that are taken off the island for disposal. There are about 800 underground garbage sucking systems used throughout the world. The garbage doesn't sit outside to rot and smell, so many other cities are researching the underground garbage tube system.

The waste arrives at a special building, where it is separated into containers.

Waste is sucked out through a network of pipes.

The Roosevelt Island pneumatic garbage collection

UNDERGROUND FARMING

About 100 feet (33 m) below London, a farm grows food for the people who live in the city. There are no pests, no noise, and no smell of rotting manure! But being underground means there's also no natural light for plants to grow.

Underground Food

The Growing Underground farm is located in an abandoned air-raid tunnel from World War II. The operation uses **hydroponic** growing and **LED** lighting systems to produce plants for food. This means the plants are grown in water or gravel without soil. Energy-efficient lights create fake sunlight for the plants. The company grows nutritious lettuces and herbs year-round and sells to local stores and restaurants. The way the food is grown and the fact that it is not shipped a long way to buyers makes this a very environmentally friendly system.

Herbs are grown ▷ under special lights in London's underground farm.

△ Vertical farming saves space by growing food in stacked layers.

Other Underground Growers

Leafy greens and lettuce also grow beneath a 26-story office tower in Stockholm, Sweden. The underground Plantagon CityFarm grows food. As an added bonus, the farm also heats the building. The heat from the LED lights used to grow plants is captured and recycled. Plants are grown hydroponically using vertical "towers" that stack them on top of each other. This makes it easier to grow a large amount of food in a small underground space. The crops are sold to people who work in the offices and to nearby restaurants.

DID YOU KNOW?

Heat recycling at Plantagon CityFarm saves 700,000 kilowatt hours of energy. The amount of money saved is enough to cover the operation's rent.

GLOSSARY

air raid An attack by airplanes during which bombs are dropped onto ground targets

aquifer Underground rock that water flows through

archaeologist Someone who studies human history by examining artifacts

architect Someone who designs buildings and other structures

bacteria Microscopic organisms, or living things, some of which cause diseases

bedrock Solid rock under loose rock

chamber pot A bowl used as a toilet and kept in the bedroom

chemicals Substances that interact with others, such as water, to purify or change them

cholera A deadly disease caused by contaminated water

decompose To rot or decay

dredged Cleaned a body of water by scooping out debris and mud

embankment A wall of earth or stone by a river that is used to prevent flooding

festered Became rotten

fossil fuels Natural fuels, such as coal or gas, that were formed millions of years ago from the remains of living things

heat exchanger A device that transfers heat from one liquid to another

hydroponic Growing plants without soil

LED Short for Light-Emitting Diode, a device that gives off light when an electric current passes through it

medieval From the Middles Ages, a period of time in Europe from 500 to 1500 C.E.

pneumatic Operated under air or gas pressure

pumping station A station where engines are powered to pump things

reservoir A large natural or artificial lake that is used as a water source

sewage system A system that transports and treats waste

slaughterhouse Places where animals were killed for meat

sluice gates Sliding gates that control the flow of water

suction Describes something that uses air to suck things up

utility Services that are useful to people, such as electricity or water

World War II A war involving the Allies (U.K, U.S., Canada, and others) against the Axis Powers (Germany, Italy, and Japan) from 1939–45

LEARNING MORE

Books

Roza, Greg, *How Do Sewers Work?* (Capstone, 2016).

Bali, Alain, *Paris Underground: The Dark Side of the City of Light* (La-Vibe Publishing, 2014).

Farley, David, *Underground Worlds: A Guide to Spectacular Subterranean Places* (Black Dog & Leventhal, 2018).

Websites

https://home.howstuffworks.com/home-improvement/plumbing/sewer3.htm
Learn more about how sewer systems work.

www.msdlouky.org/programs/whenuflush/homeplumbing.html
Find out how water reaches your home and where your waste goes.

www.smithsonianmag.com/travel/five-fascinating-sewer-tours-180955201/
Dive into this story about sewer tours.

INDEX